ella zelensky

breaking enigma

ella zelensky

breaking enigma

ella zelensky

the best game of hide and seek is seeking the wisdoms that hide in the most unexpected of places. to search for the subliminal in the mundane. and the profound in the ordinary.

© Ella Zelensky, 2024. All Rights Reserved

breaking enigma

ella zelensky

also by ella zelensky

Divine Decree

Little *Dreamer*

At First *Light*

breaking enigma

breaking enigma

ella zelensky

chapter one: despondency

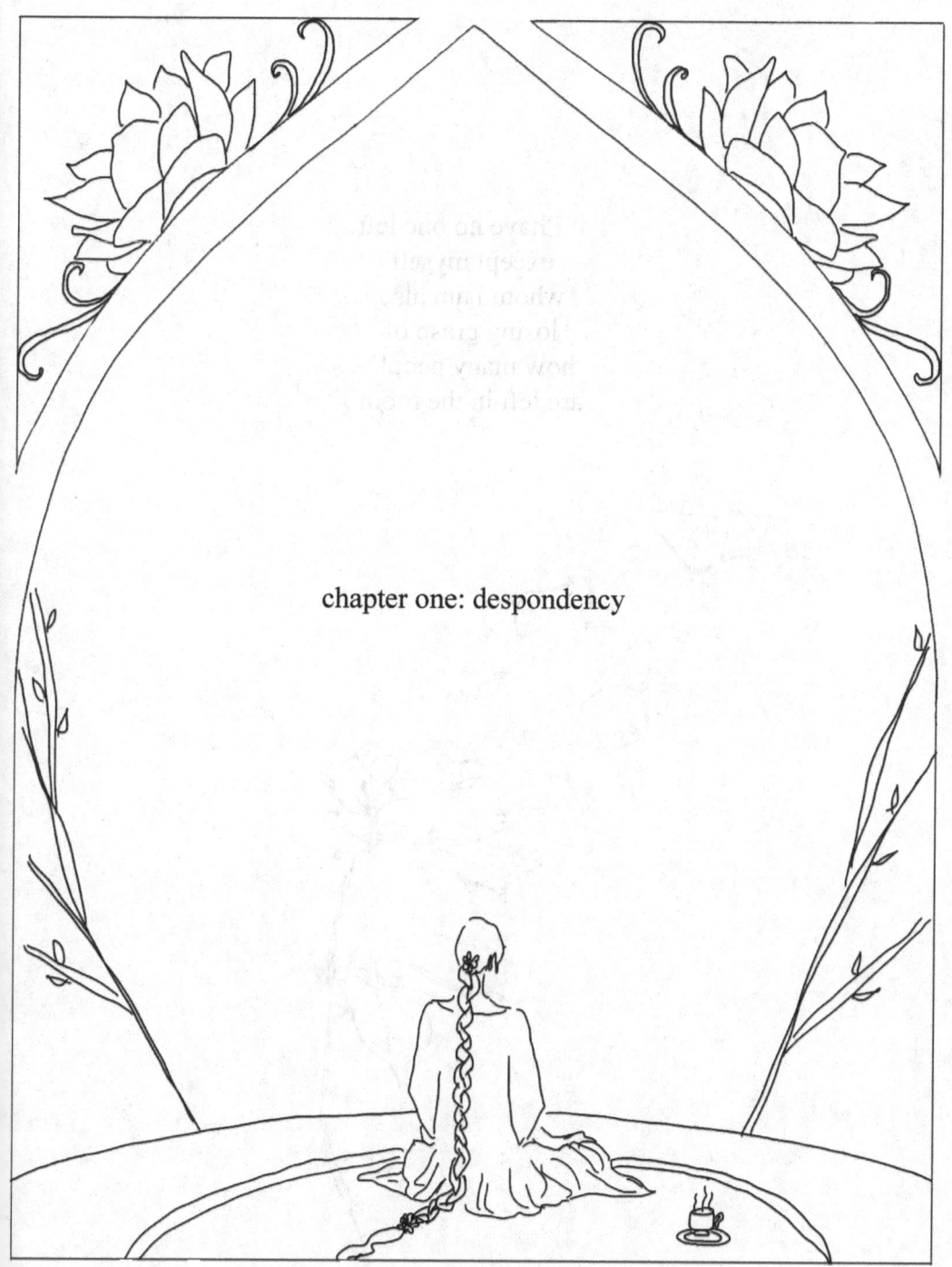

if i have no one left
except myself
whom i am also
losing grasp of
how many people
are left in the room

tearing yourself apart
will not bring them back
do not give any more
energy to the one who
is already gone

breaking enigma

this whole time
was it a world
you built that i
thought i was
dancing in

i fell into
the pond
and arose in alternate
universes
like passing through
portals over and over

breaking enigma

it was as
fast as the
blowing out
of a candle for
it all to end
for the room to
go dark in
an instant
and never see
your light again

you weep no tears
you are not human

you cause the damage
wherever you go
and force us all to
restore it with mops
and buckets

ella zelensky

i felt like
the shower water
that had fallen
into the drain

breaking enigma

you pull apart puzzles
after people have spent
so long putting them
together
you undo all
their hard work on
piecing themselves
together again

you broke me
like plates being
thrown on
the floor

how many pages
do i really want
you to take up
when i could be
writing of better
things

the colour scale
of the world
changes when
others hurt you
the whole world
suddenly feels
unreal

you rob people
of their happiness like money
but still wonder why you are
broke

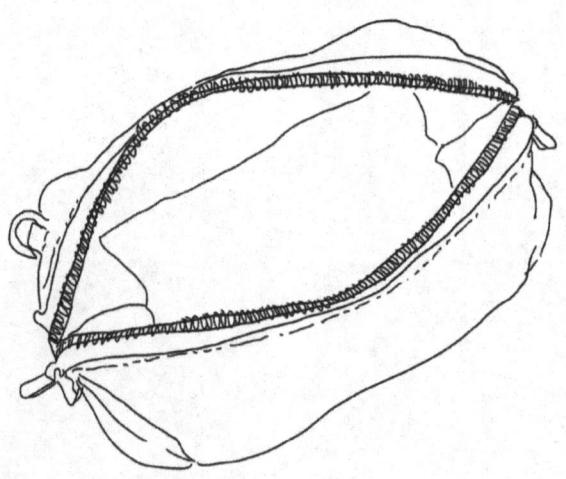

ella zelensky

i don't want to
be swept up
by arms
that intend not
to embrace me
with love

i cried so hard
the clouds collected
my tears
and travelled to
rain them upon you

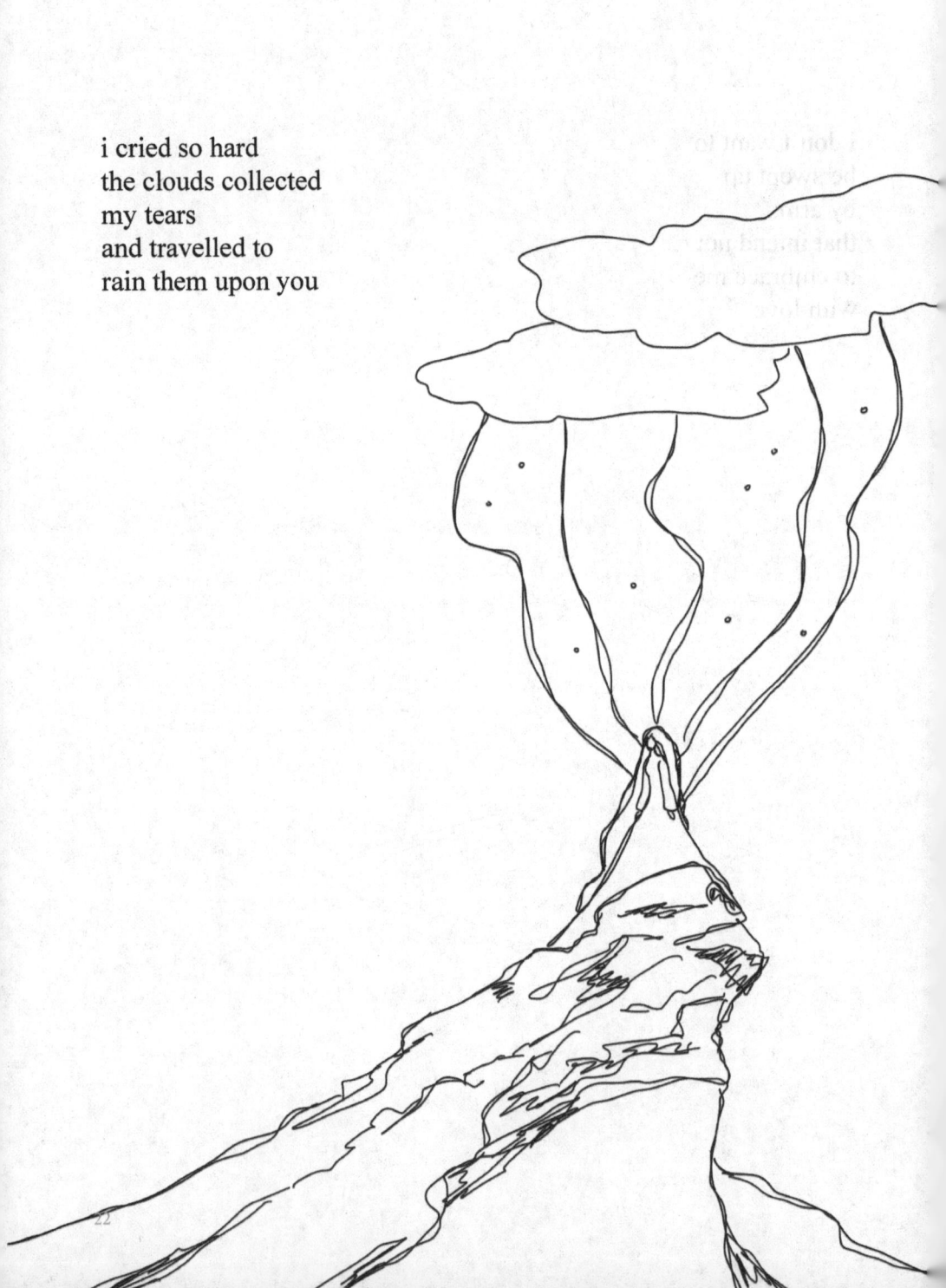

just because
i held the door
open for you
doesn't mean
i've excused how
you treated me

i am not stronger
because of you
i am stronger
because of what
you did
you do not take
credit for my growth

sometimes all i want is for
my heart and mind to be friends

i missed you
until i no longer
missed the feeling
of missing you

ella zelensky

it seems these days
i become more tired
from thinking than doing

the pillow does not judge
when you cry
the pillow did far better
than many people did

ella zelensky

they will never understand
they will never understand
they will never understand
until it happens to them

being at war
with ourselves
can have the effect
of putting others at
war around us

someone has
threaded my lips
downward
wound my eyes
halfway shut
i can't help it
it's written all over
my face

you are a strange one
begging for sympathy
and praise when you
aren't getting it
anywhere else
you are a cruel one
for making me feel
like we were friends
until the very end
i should have known
this was coming
that you would stop
talking to me because
i wasn't satisfying
your ego anymore
but i was too kind
too sweet
to prepare for this
dead end

ella zelensky

the thing was
i wasn't dead
when you
rolled me away
into the ocean
so i laid out there
barely alive but
still awake

perhaps my heart
knows something
my mind hasn't
caught up with yet

**you made me want
the sun to never
come back**

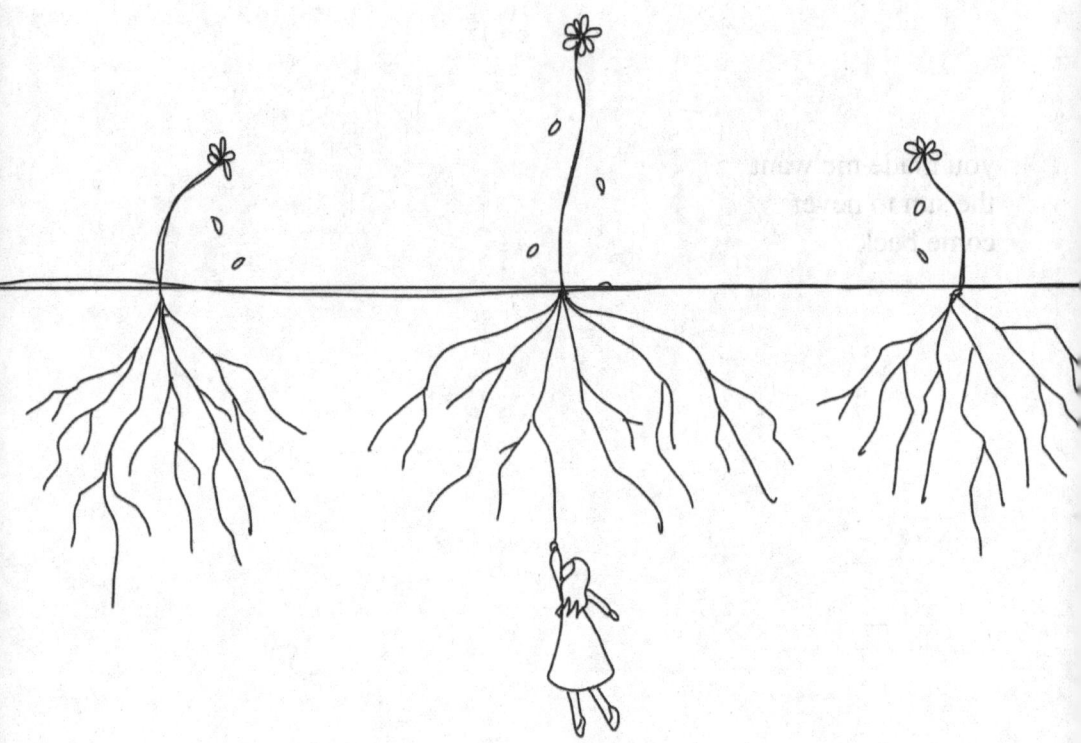

i felt like i was being buried
not underground but in
the air all around me
perhaps that's what they mean
by suffocating on the air
when something is troubling you

sometimes sadness is a choice
to be bound to negative hypotheticals

i'm hurting
but this time
because i've
wronged myself

ella zelensky

you can't stand tall
when you're dragging
your past with you
by your back

when i stared
into the mirror
i saw the eyes
of my enemy
the one person
who shouldn't
have been
was staring back
at me
threatening to
claim my body
heart and mind
if i didn't
save her myself

ella zelensky

in our lifetime we keep
far more inside our heads
then we ever say out loud
and we take to the grave with
us thoughts we never shared

a clock ticked in place
of my beating heart

ella zelensky

standing under
the sun is
too exposing
too painful
that is why
i live in the cold
for it is better
to be numb than
it is to get burnt

**fear feels like a like a colony of ants
sprawling all over my mind**

the bird in my heart
aches with longing
to fly into the open
sky above me

breaking enigma

being calm will take
me to the surface
being anxious will
pull me under

ella zelensky

tears cleanse your eyes
to help you see things
with more clarity

breaking enigma

i thought i
had to go
running to
dark places
to bring back
powerful poetry
i thought i
had to revisit
the past to make
my impact last
to be inspiring
now i know
that the best
poetry isn't always
written because
of pain
because many
poems are written
after the end
of torrential rain

ella zelensky

there was a peace
underlying my sorrow
for i wept over
a love not lost
but a love experienced

even in darkness
do our eyes eventually
adjust to find our way out

ella zelensky

mourning can be happy
when you celebrate someone

when you cry a river
cross it to the other side
your lungs are your life jacket
and your heart the compass

ella zelensky

it took me years to love
the solace of the moon
as equally as the embrace
of the sun

it was the same place but a different version of me who used to walk through it. back then, my physical body would trudge through the grass, but it pulled a shadow that kept falling to its knees and wanting to stay down. back then, the sun was silver and not gold, the grass blue and not green. the world was a discontinued video game haunting the characters who were left behind but could never leave the decaying machine that trapped them in its story. now, i had found the secret door back to life. now, i had stumbled out of the once locked closet. now, the sun was a stunning gold that warmed everything it touched. nature was green, dotted with flowers of all colours of the rainbow. there was nothing of me to drag along. how strange that the same place can carry two different emotions. that an older me can smile walking through it because she once raged with desperate survival, pounding her fists on a door that didn't open for her for years. now, she danced and thew her arms in the air. she could sing and laugh and know that she was alive. and wanted to be.

ella zelensky

breaking enigma

chapter two: victory

my lonely days
have subsided
for now i have
sided with myself
i am my own friend
until the very end
the first one to
hold my hand
because i understand
myself the best out
of everybody

if it is an inevitable part of our lives
then we were designed to withstand it

climbing up
from rock bottom
is a skill that
stays with you

there was a piece
of me in a book
i wrote in almost
ten years ago
and i keep
her diary
on my shelf
instead of throwing
her into the bin
because she
wrote for
her future
who lives now

beautiful things are coming
you may not see them from here
but they are waving at
you from a distance
they are eager for your arrival

breaking enigma

often what is considered impossible
is only a choice away from it becoming
true

ella zelensky

they fought with chains
but you fought with brains
because when you
confine the body
the mind remains

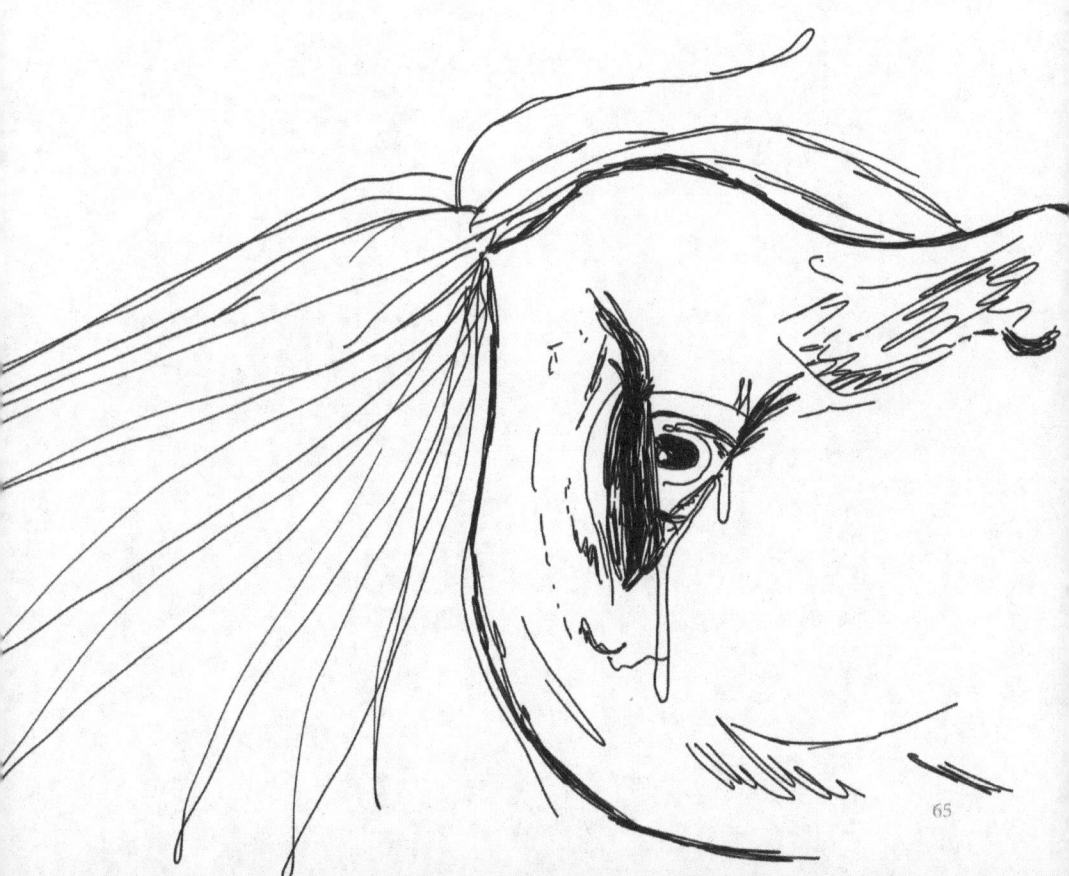

breaking enigma

the ashes are not
my burial place
indeed i will fly again
with the wings you were
convinced you broke

i'm sorry but
i did not give
you my
permission to
bully me
like that

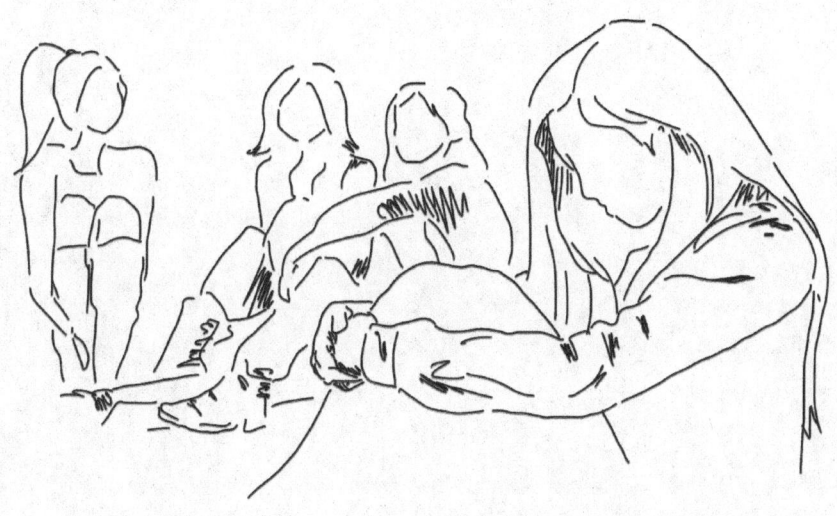

breaking enigma

you will not carry
into my calendar
for next year
i'm sick of waiting
for a friend who was
never really here

ella zelensky

i was of pure heart when
i entered this world
and i want to be of pure
heart when i leave it
i don't want the darkness
of this world to annihilate
my soul

i had to fall
to learn how
to fly
to embrace
what living
means to no
longer fear
the day
i die
to experience
happiness to
realise it too
can cry
and to appreciate
fate without
being immobilised
by why

ella zelensky

the crack in the glass
is elegance
this wilting dance
this fragmentation
behind the scenes
is elegance

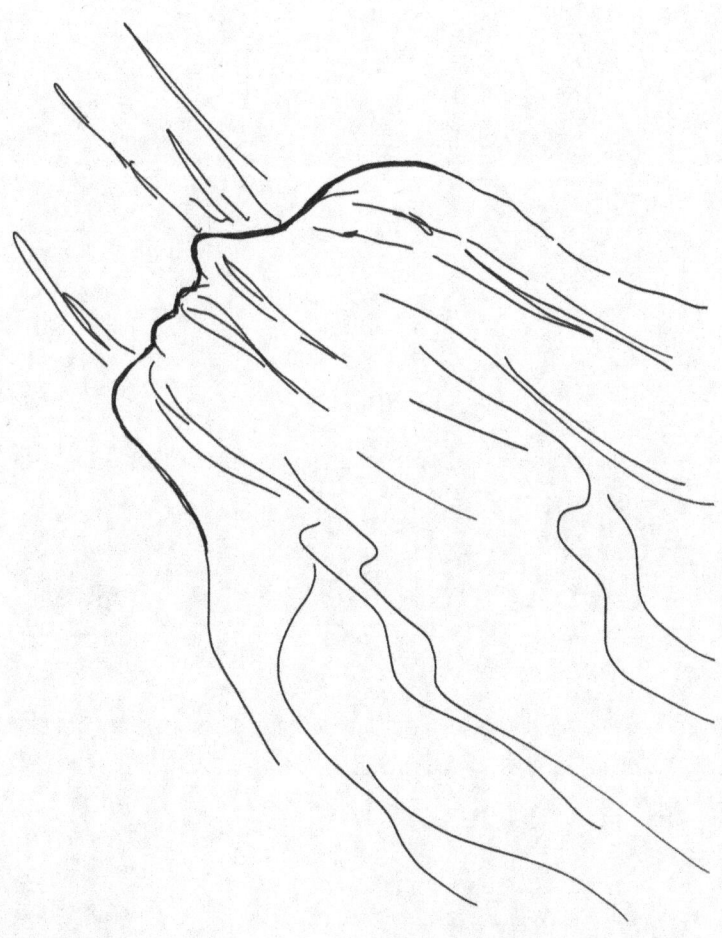

breaking enigma

we don't have forever
but that should be our inspiration

i have avoided mirrors
because my subconscious self
is afraid of watching me
realise i am worthy of
fitting a crown on my head
my subconscious self is afraid
that i will connect stunningly
with the gaze of my own eyes
and abandon my old narrative

just make the change
and the future will too

i thought the life
i longed for belonged
to a different universe
until patience revealed
its existence to me here

breaking enigma

flowers need the sun to bloom
do not be afraid of stepping into the light

ella zelensky

once i found
love
in my inner
world
i dove into it
like water
and became
one with it

make your mind
the home you love
to come back to

anything could happen i said with fear
but anything could happen you said with hope

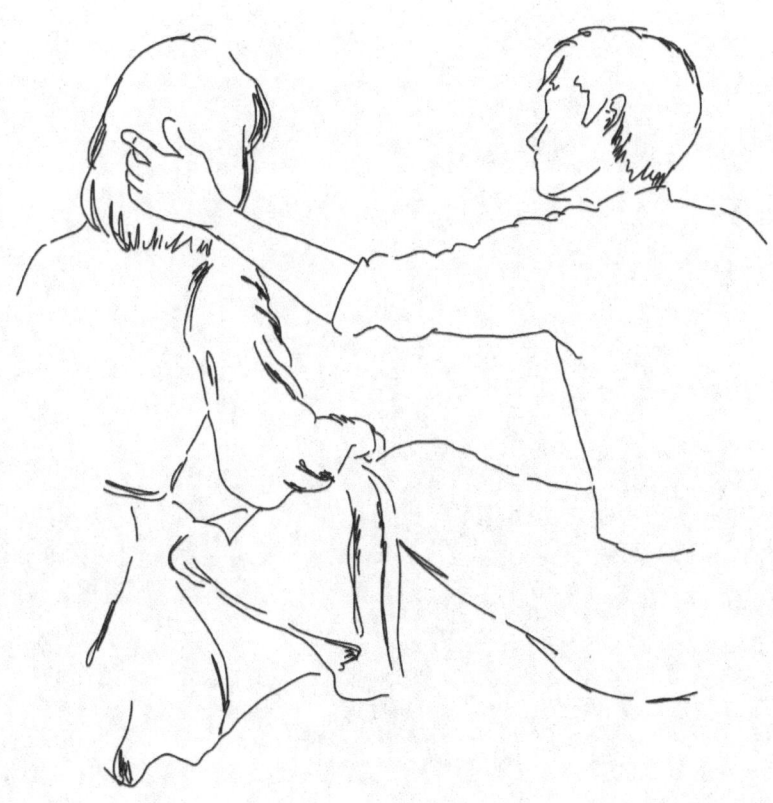

it's not too good to be true –
there is goodness in this world
and my love, it is true

ella zelensky

you were right
i wasn't meant for this
i was meant for
something far greater

breaking enigma

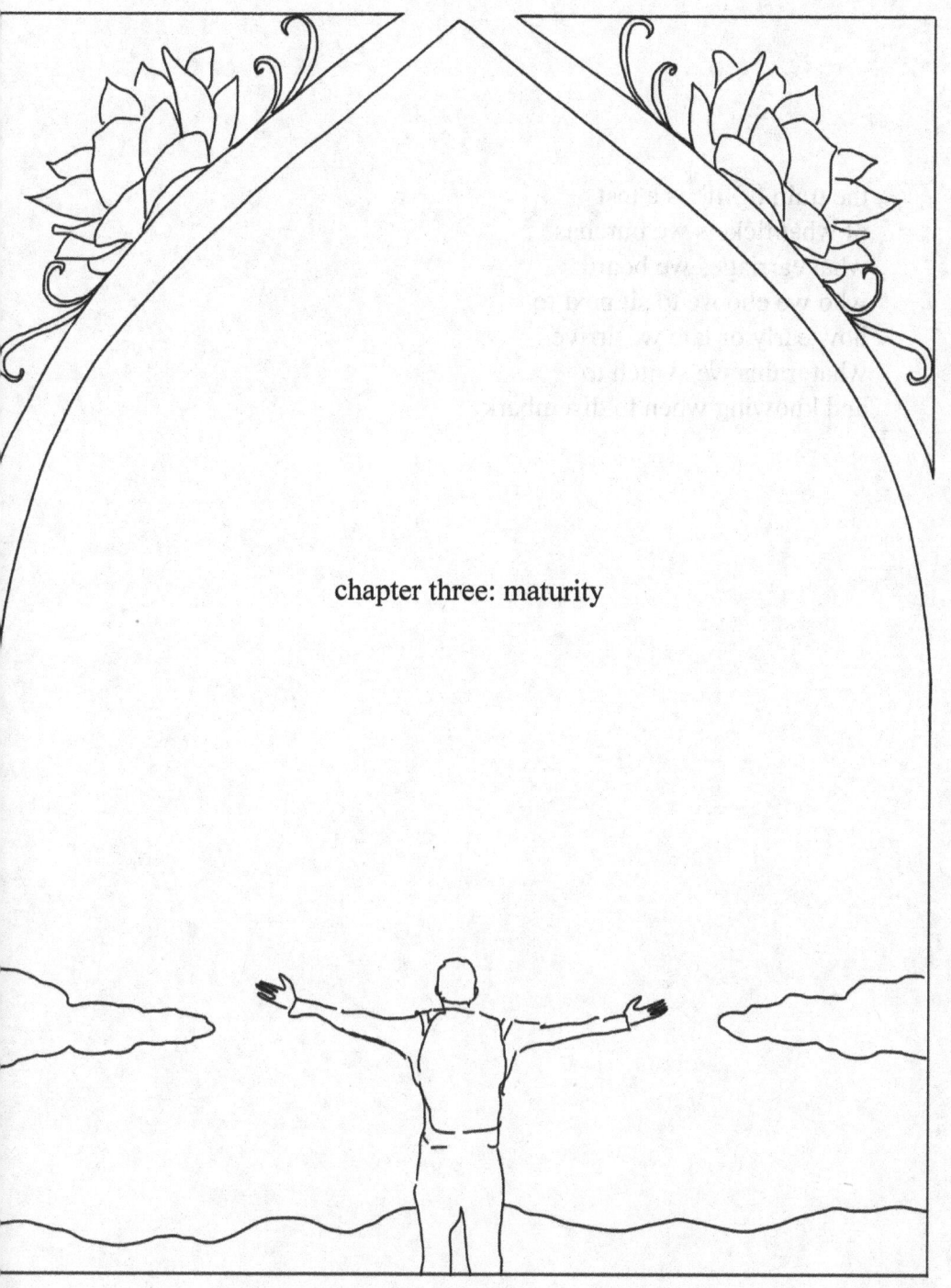

chapter three: maturity

the train of life is a test
of what tickets we purchase
what carriages we board
who we choose to sit next to
how early or late we arrive
what trains we switch to
and knowing when to disembark

ella zelensky

life is a commitment
made up of many
other commitments
to avoid commitment
is to avoid life

we have become desperate
in our attempts to avoid
every possible way of
experiencing what it
means to be human

**your existence isn't meant
to be lived passively**

breaking enigma

one thing is for certain
and that is the inevitability
of the uncertain

**failing at something
is winning at learning**

breaking enigma

do not wound yourself
to perpetuate self evasion

ella zelensky

i used to be afraid of crowds
until i realised there was no
tougher crowd than my own
mind

breaking enigma

experience shields you more than avoidance
for experiences teaches us what shield we
must make to avoid the same mistake

it is possible to learn
how to learn if only you
allow the uncomfortable in

some people will learn their lesson in life
and some people will learn their lesson in death

if your whole existence is anger
you cannot complain of waiting
for a happiness you will deflect anyway

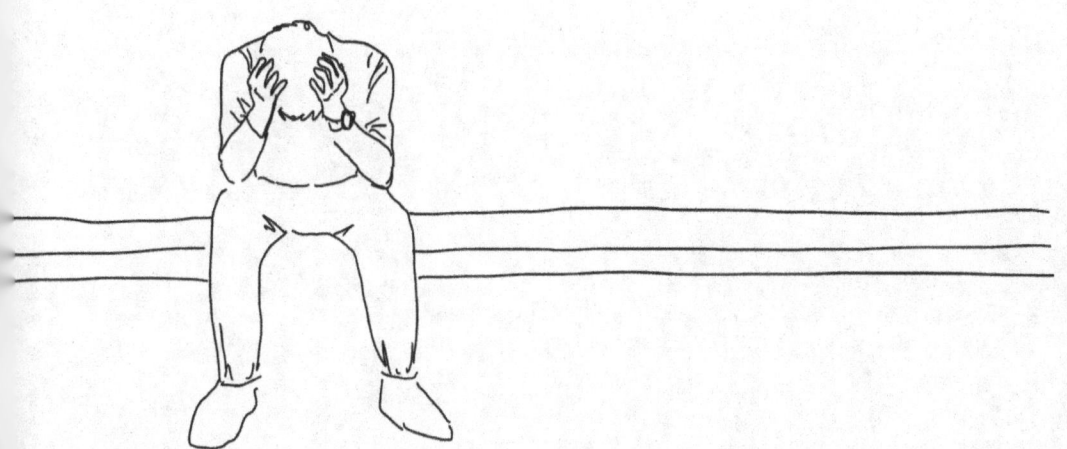

breaking enigma

you say you have
next to nothing
as you stand next
to everything

ella zelensky

why have ears when the only opinions
you listen to are those between them

breaking enigma

you avoid certain topics because
they make it hard to avoid yourself

we see reflections
of ourselves in others
and run away because
we weren't ready
to see them

breaking enigma

you disappeared
when i stopped
affirming your
behaviour

my heart is not
a free trial

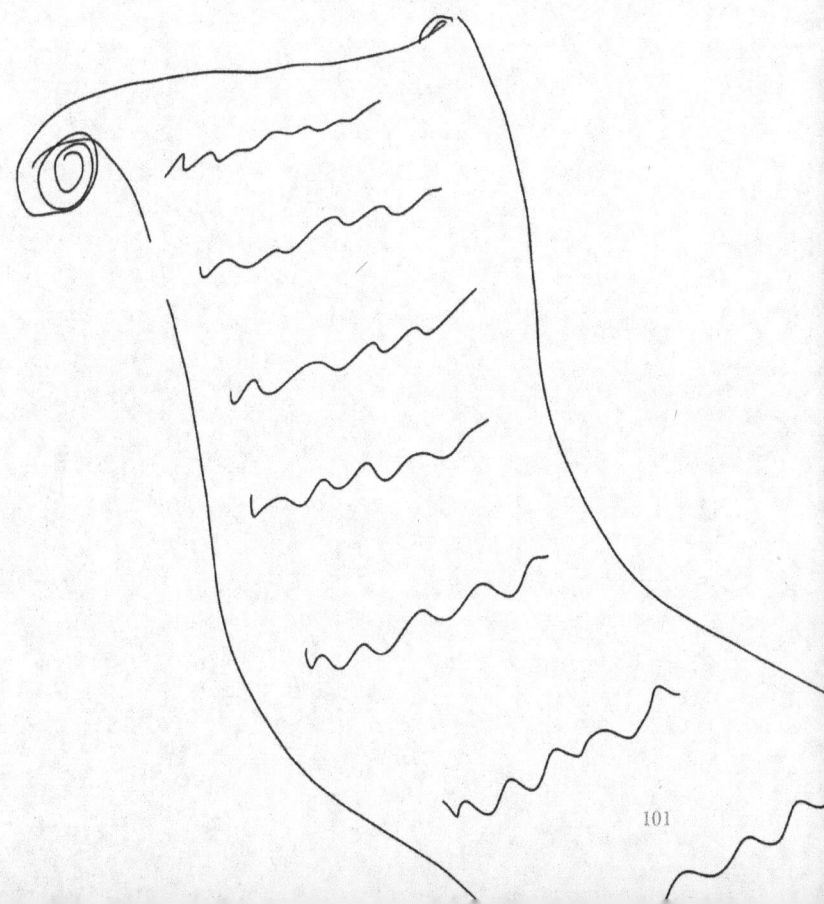

they don't perceive
what you mean
because they are
operating within a
world that can't
perceive further
dimensions

i realised there was
a weight on
my shoulders
because you were
standing on them
and still
the thing you were
searching for
remained out of reach

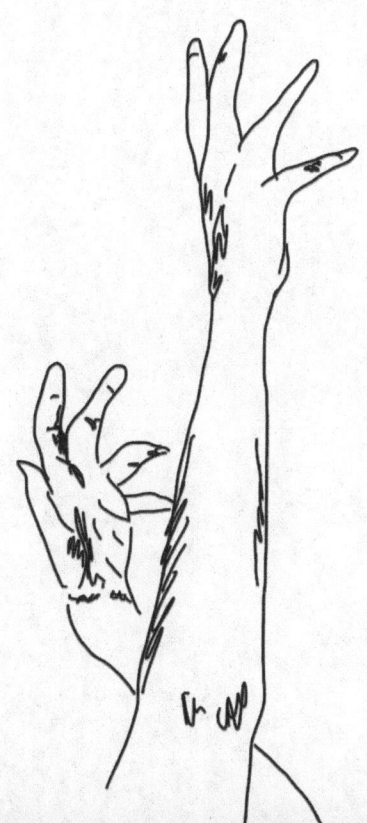

it takes selflessness
to love for others
what you do not yet
have for yourself

praise in private
is often more
meaningful
and gratifying
than publicly
declared praise
it means someone
has personal
appreciation they
want to give to
you directly

we were the dirt beneath your feet. we were the ones who came to be forgotten, because you buried us so deep people forgot about us. you made a mess of us and were so afraid of people figuring things out. that you had to clean that mess by packing it away frantically in a cupboard where no one would find us. you lied and continue to lie through your grinning teeth about the purity of your character. you boast a good reputation built on the bones of those you knocked over, if you even have a reputation at all. people respect you. people speak good of you. people revere you as a friend, as a leader. but you sacrificed many in the process to advertise that image. you were never a tidy person. you caused damage you never cared to fix. you formulated stories that went all over the place. you caused heartbreak and refused to collect any of the pieces, shoving them back at us to put back together. and you relied on us to stay silent. you liked it. it was disgusting.

when one is afraid of the truth getting out, they run to everyone hastily to establish a story to demonise the other person. but when you are the one who said the truth, you find no reason to hide anything, because the truth has nothing to hide. i didn't clap for you that day as you crossed the stage, and you know why. but i wish you healing, even if you never wish healing for me. if ever i were to desire an apology, i wouldn't want it face to face in verbal form. if ever you do apologise, apologise by never repeating what you did to me and all your friends at school. that will be your redemption.

i was quiet and knew
you were loud
but did not
unfortunately it
is the loud
who are perceived to
be informed
and the quiet oblivious

sometimes what we hear
distracts us from what we see

people will give you bait
and snatch you up
in their net
this is what happens
when you hang out
where things are shallow

breaking enigma

the guilty blame
defame
and shame
the victim
walks away
because they
refuse to play
their game

nothing may have been said
but the situation has
intuitively been read

yes revenge
is sweet
revenge is kind
revenge is letting
a lesson to be taught
with time
in this sense
revenge is no
longer revenge
but rather
an invitation to
change

greatness in status
has no weight
when there exists
no goodness in
your heart

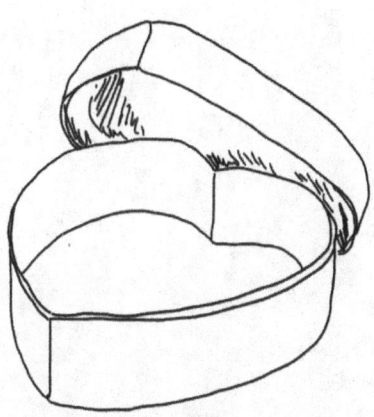

breaking enigma

the more you twist the narrative
the harder it is to stay consistent
with it without the truth slipping
out absentmindedly
that is what happened without
you noticing
now all eyes are on you

sometimes you have
to rock the boat
to ultimately stabilise it

breaking enigma

**forget enacting the verb
you couldn't even describe
the noun**

ella zelensky

you didn't fit
the criteria
because you
didn't fit
the mould
you argued
the unexpected
instead of
writing what
you were told

breaking enigma

often the most important step
you must take is stepping away
from the situation

ella zelensky

**when our five senses
have failed us
our intuition cries
that it knew all along**

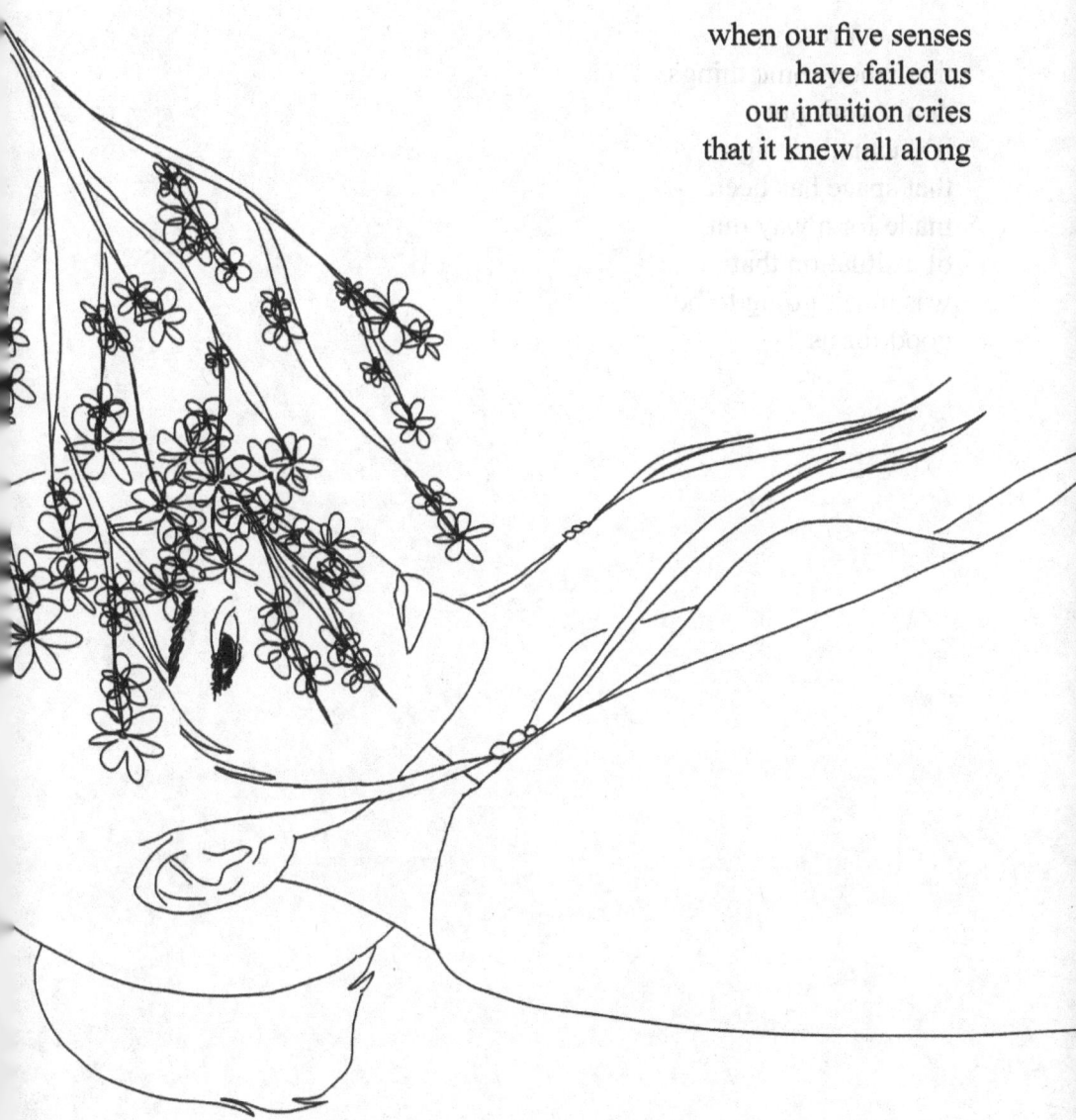

breaking enigma

we must realise
that when some things
don't work out
it's actually a sign
that space has been
made for a way out
of a situation that
was never going to be
good for us

to contemplate
successfully
is not to find
every answer
but rather to
find contentment
in the extent to
which we can
find one
even if it
is seemingly
nothing

breaking enigma

you walked with me
so i would know how
to on my own
through this i have
learnt that wherever
i go
i will never go alone

your friendship
with yourself is
the only friendship
you can't physically lose

breaking enigma

as i sat down on the park bench
i simultaneously sat down with myself
and so began the conversation with
my soul that lead me to the beginning
of my internal happiness

ella zelensky

breaking enigma

breaking enigma

the people you hurt
whose name you
can't remember
will be the people
who will return to
remind you of what
they are

ella zelensky

you came to buy her
but she was the one
to pay the greater price

breaking enigma

they let the tides take them
because it was the only
thing that would

ella zelensky

she took the hits
so her sister would
never know what
punches were like

the contradiction of
marking territory
whilst also being open

ella zelensky

in an already lonely universe
it is a tragedy that in a world
of billions humanity too
remains alone

breaking enigma

**love is to hold someone's hand
control is to hold someone's wrist**

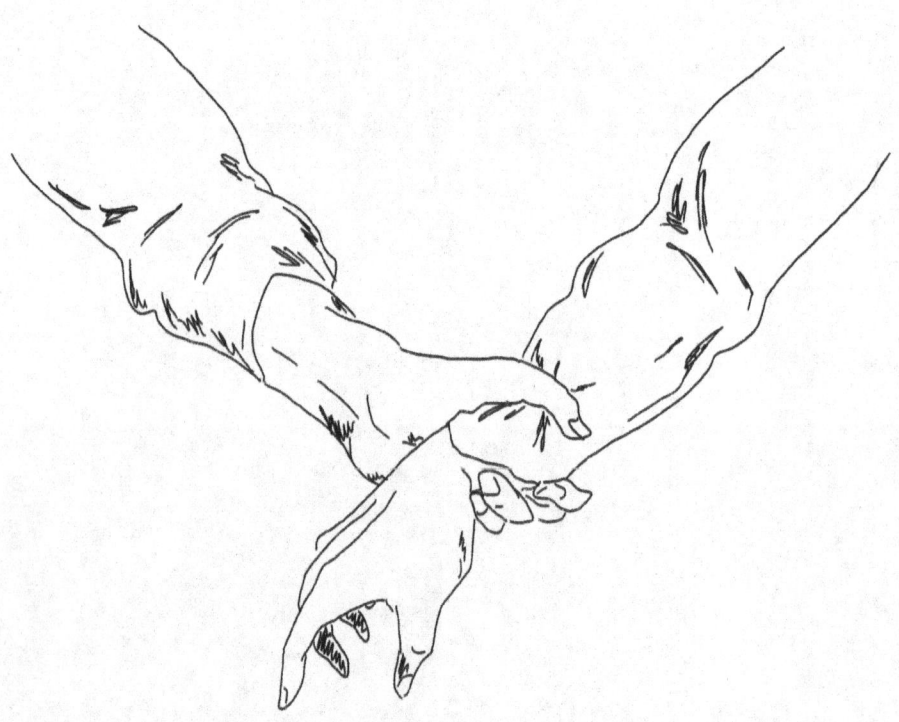

just because
they can't read
words doesn't
mean they can't
read a situation

there was so much
fear and sorrow
on that lifeboat that
even it couldn't keep
the people on it
afloat

ella zelensky

we shall have
a big house
and beds to
sleep in
windows that
overlook pretty
places
with plenty of
spaces for you
and me and the
rest of our family
painted walls
and decorated halls
we shall host
elegant balls and
dance underneath
diamonds
until we awaken
from its light and
find ourselves back
where we started
with a small house
and no beds to
sleep in
windows that overlook
famine and suffering
with little space for
me and you and the
rest of what is left
of our family
decaying walls
and no halls
to host elegant balls
nor to dance beneath
what money can afford
because our reality
can't afford our dreams
and in the end
we will die with them

breaking enigma

if the only way
to live my dreams
forever is to die
in my sleep they thought
then i will surrender
myself

ella zelensky

how are we awarding
to leaders our votes
who encourage communities
to be at each other's throats

one mother can see all
the world's children
as her own when they
cry for someone

to give one's life
for the chance
of another's is
one of the most
beautiful and
heartbreaking
exchanges many
in humankind
have to make

breaking enigma

how curious a reality
that whilst some cities
are obliterated by bombs
others are celebrated with
fireworks

ella zelensky

diversity is one of the most
natural things in this world
do not be afraid of your
global siblings

and they died
so that their
corpses could
create the bridge
their community
could cross
as a grim road
to a better life
or at the very least
a chance for one

ella zelensky

they threw the match
walked into
the roaring flame
and burnt with
their tears
standing as still
as a statue
expressionless

breaking enigma

the human thinks itself superior
but even the butterfly flies
while the human cannot

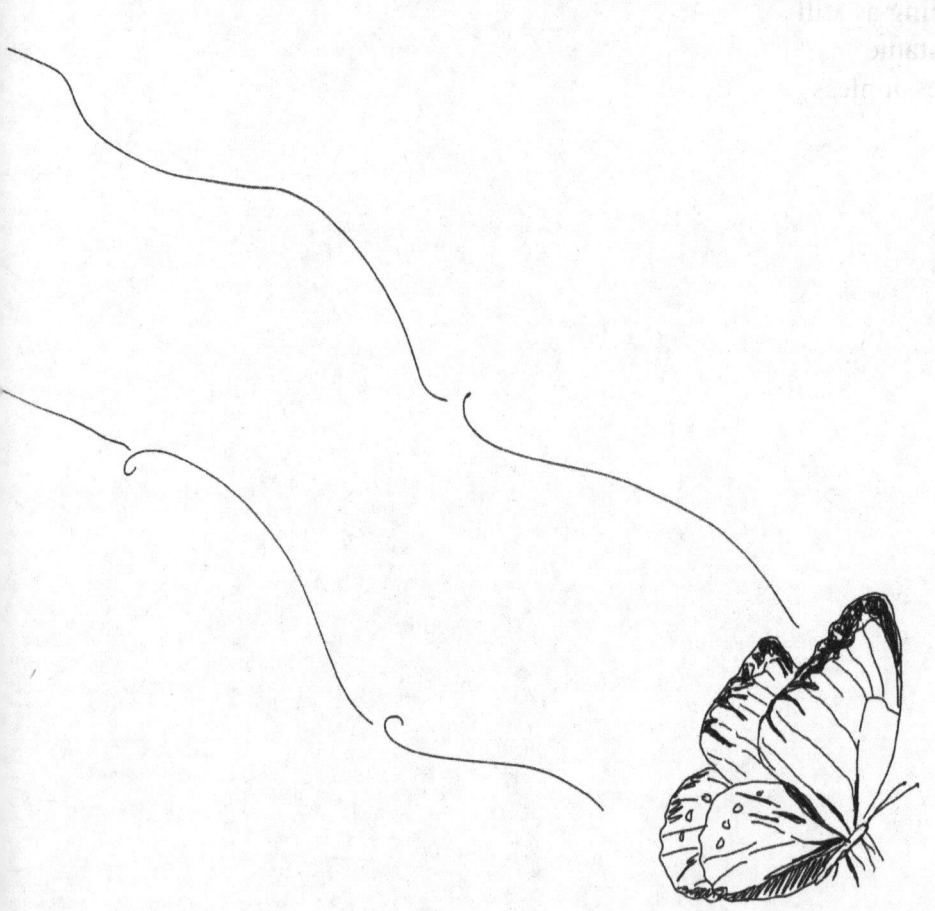

**lightning can strike anyone
you are not invincible to
some of the worst of fates**

breaking enigma

how terrible
that people will
tailor things
at the cost
of their bodies
for people in
foreign countries
who claim they
buy what they make
because they can't
afford anything else

ella zelensky

we are applauding
things in this world
we don't even fully
understand

breaking enigma

when you dare to
speak the truth
you are hunted
killed
and displayed for it

the world is just
becoming one big
unlearnt lesson

breaking enigma

the oppressors
will fall with the
towers they built
when the earth
shakes beneath them
and just like
their towers
they will hit the
ground and turn
to nothing greater
than dust

ella zelensky

they left flags
along the path
so all their people
could follow them
to freedom too

rise, my beloved ones
it is your time
you are not lost in history

i found a film
encasing movements
of you
and found a
movie projector
to see you come to life
i found a secret letter
kept in a bedside drawer
you wrote to a lover
many years ago whom you
eloped with
in a beautiful dress
that blew like a parachute
in the wind
you held hands tightly
and ran through the tall
fields of sugar cane
the euphoria of disobedience
and the truest love
flowing between your
intertwined fingers
i found you around a sunlit
corner in the house
with him picking you up
twirling with you in his
arms in one spin
and with your baby in his
hands the next

(part 1)

breaking enigma

the kitchen called me to it
where i saw you feeding
one another in affection
laughing and holding one
another's faces
until there were only two
to cook for
the baby cried gently
for a mother who died
delivering her
the baby was a girl
she grew up watching her
father watch movies about
forbidden love and sugar cane
fields and parachutes
and morning sunlight
she thought it was beautiful
but somehow familiar
so close
yet eternally
out of reach

(part 2)

ella zelensky

sometimes a
display of
real love is
too real for
the eyes
to change their
mind over

breaking enigma

the invention of the camera came
with disaster and miracle
for on the one hand
it captured what wasn't real
and on the other
it captured what truly was

we all want love
but we must learn
to give it too
imagine a world
stitched back
together by love
we must change
from there's nothing
i'd ever do for you
to there's nothing
i wouldn't do

ella zelensky

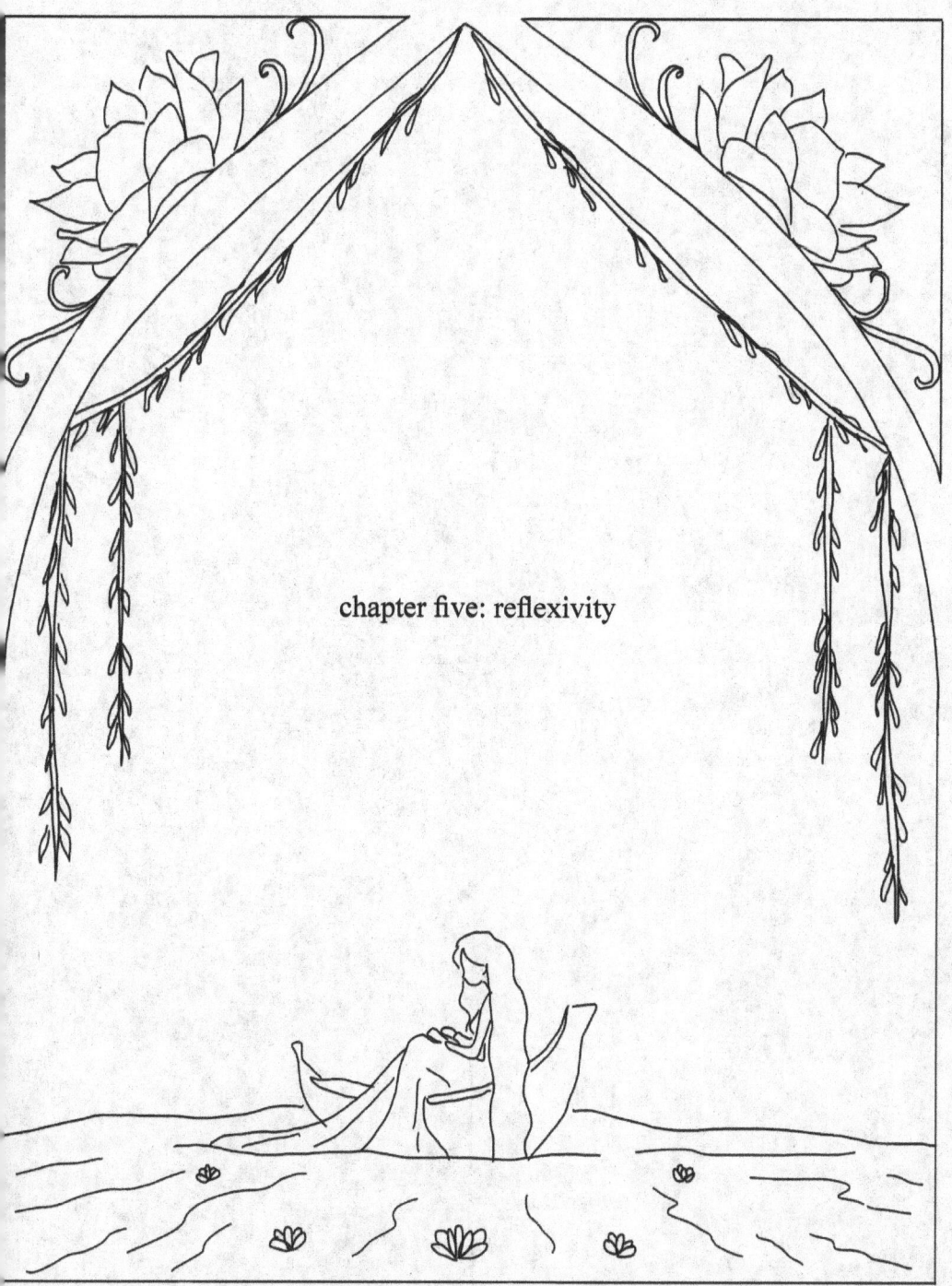

chapter five: reflexivity

breaking enigma

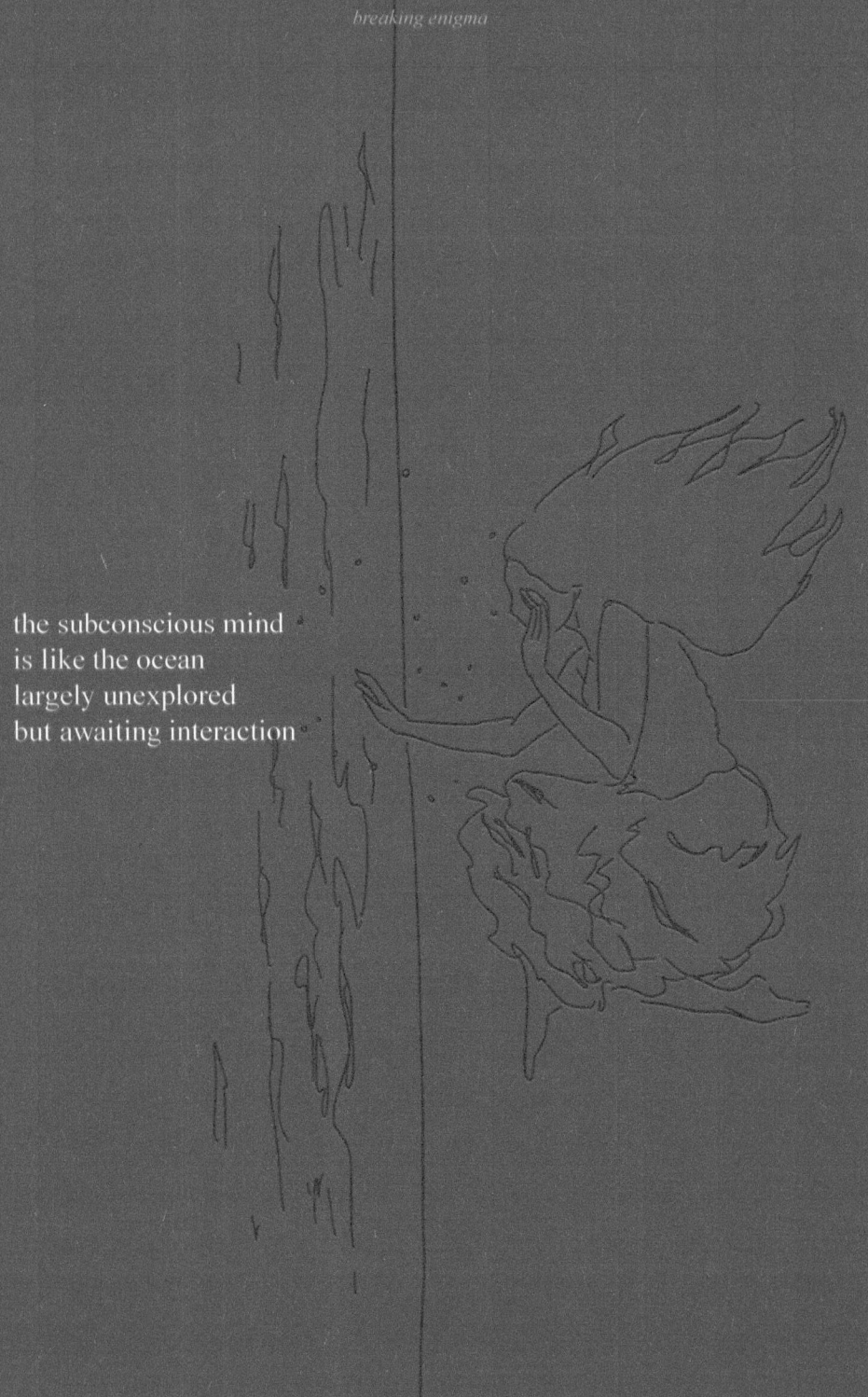

the subconscious mind
is like the ocean
largely unexplored
but awaiting interaction

i dreamt i was in a chamber of glass
forced to contemplate
i stared at my reflection until
i heard the sound of twinkling
and was set free with newfound clarity

breaking enigma

dreams are sensical
even directory
if dissected carefully

unlike the camera
the mind doesn't
run out of storage
when the eye
captures memorable
moments
it is the best camera
human beings
can afford

breaking enigma

there are stars in
your eyes
when you cry
in them i see
a whole universe
it is right there
in front of me
waiting
and yet your soul
keeps it far away
out of reach
from anyone
who attempts to
get close to it
and therefore
closer to you

then you allowed your eyes to be a door
and not just a window into your soul

breaking enigma

we exist in worlds
within worlds
within worlds
but folded within
its complexity is
also a hidden simplicity
waiting to be touched
by the fingertips
of those who
look for it

ella zelensky

sitting on the swing
amidst all the kids
running in the park
my feet could touch
the ground
where once they
could not
the trees that used to
excite me because of
how tall they were
to climb
were now empty of
adventure and challenge
the kids and i were in
the exact same place
and yet we saw it so
differently
i tried to enjoy swinging
higher and higher
into the air
but gravity wanted to pull
me back down
my adult brain wanted
to pull me back down
so i got up and left

breaking enigma

but they're all going
in that direction
the child insisted
the elder knelt to
his knees and said
the blind follow the
blind knowing not
that the leader is
blind themselves
so be not like the
followers
but of your own mind
the way we are going
is fine because we
are not distracted by
a deceptive end
but rather
a conscious journey
to the place we need

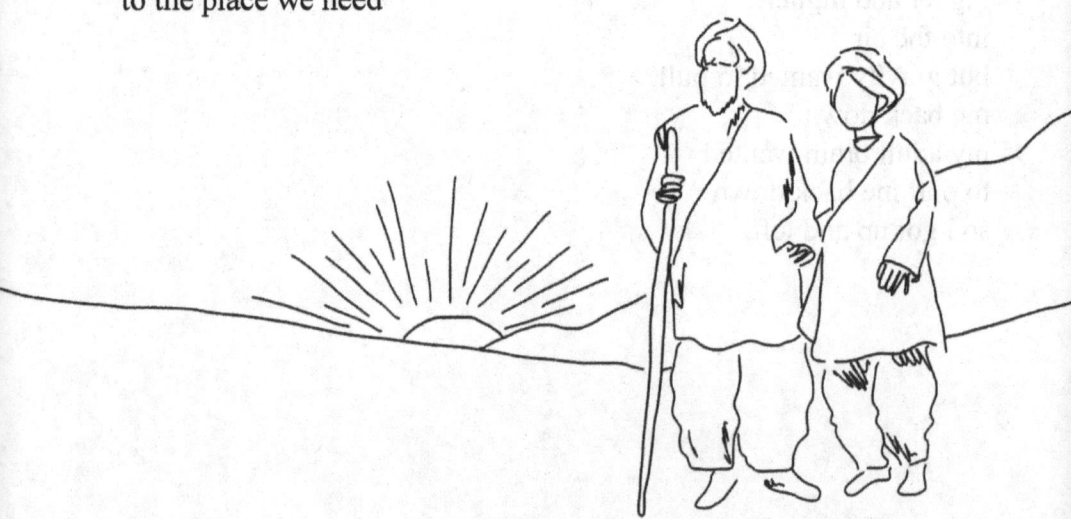

ella zelensky

i have learnt to spin with the whirlwinds
and find clarity in the chaos

the quill
and the paper
are in love
for the paper waits
to be imprinted
by the quill's eloquent
words whilst the
quill waits
for its words
to be wrapped
up in the
paper's embrace
it is the mutual
love letter bound
in secrecy
upon the rolling
of the scroll
the exchange
unknown to all
but them

ella zelensky

the moon crackled
like thunder as it
obliterated and rained
down slowly in what
would be the final
night sky we would see
chaos then ensued
hundreds of thousands
of people running
in all directions
until a second wave
of ocean plummeted
over them
permeating through
the landscape
to claim more
higher ground was
useless
for the end of time
would spare no one
terrified of being
dismembered or
choked to death
we held the hands of
those we loved
and if not possible
those we had to learn
to love in the moment
for both a terrible and
enlightening end
was upon us
the conjunction of awakening
and the final death

as the night
got darker
so did my
sadness
until rivers
of light
cascaded
my way from
all around me
lifted into the air
and showed
me what it
means to
hold on
until morning

ella zelensky

i am a small
being in a big
world
i am called bravery
i am called adventure
i am love
leaping on
lily pads
and waking
the flowers with
good morning
i am called defiance
i am called dreamer
i am joyous
the melody fades
softly as the sunlight
consumes me
and i dance slowly
in a big world
as a small being
with a heart big
enough to love my
way through
all things

dear winter
you are beautiful
as you are
the summer sun
may warm everyone
but you teach
people how to
do this themselves
you bring candles
out of shelves
and show that even
the cold snow melts
to reveal life anew
my dear winter
the people who say
they hate you
don't appreciate
how your weather
brings everyone
together
so do not fret that
people play favourites
with seasons
because for others
there is an endless
list of reasons
why you inspire them
to see beauty even in
the coldest of times
for it does not signal
an end
but rather
makes way for a
new beginning

ella zelensky

over the bridge
we go
hand in hand
into pastel
wonderland
where flowers
of all kinds
grow

breaking enigma

fairy lights and
fireworks blur
and rain down
like stars falling
down to earth
just for us

ella zelensky

when you laughed
the trees and birds
woke up
stillness began
swirling again
every
colour on
earth intensified
and although you
weren't watching
others as you did
the whole world was
watching you

breaking enigma

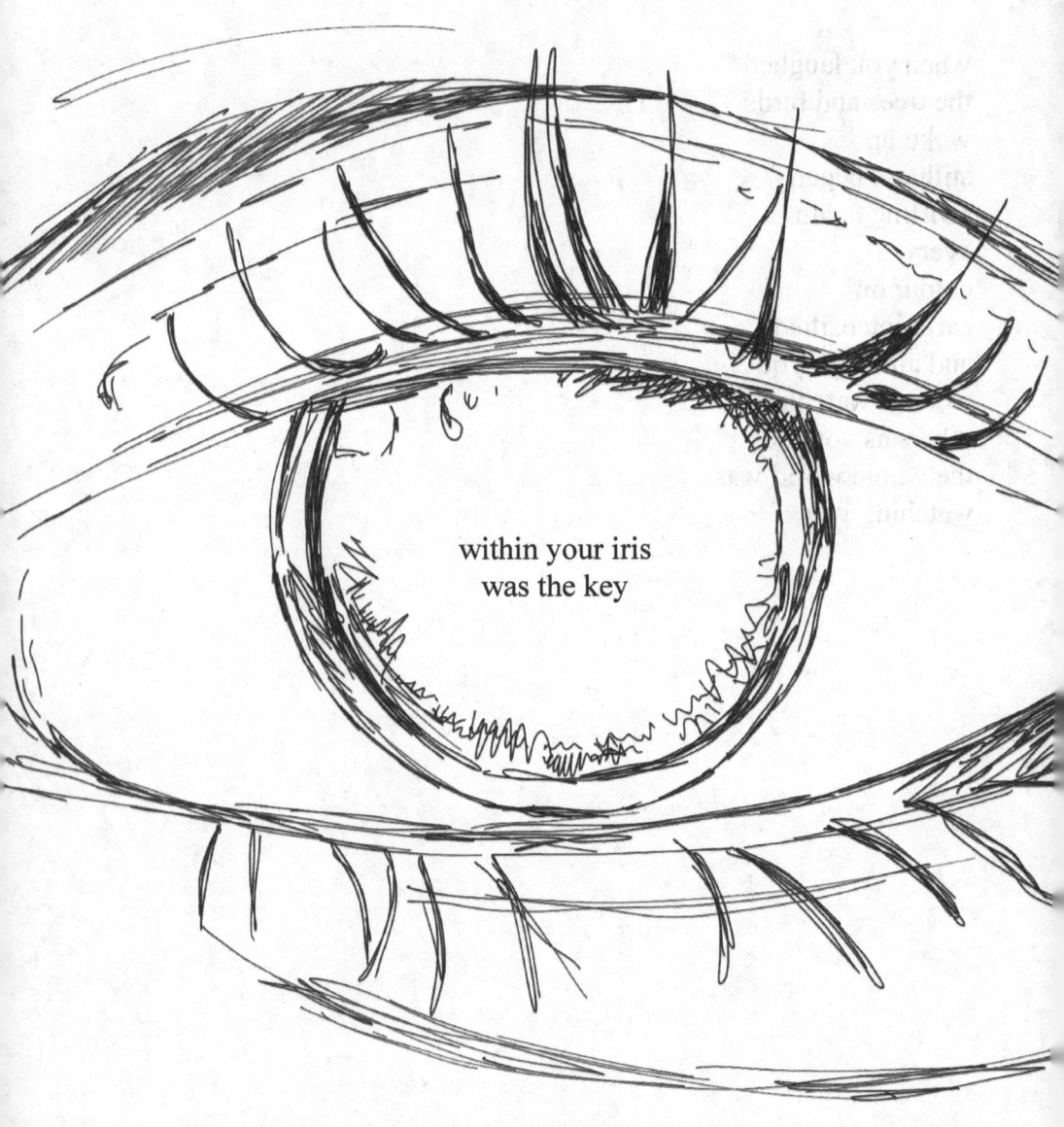

do you observe how they
dance in the air
and are both unseen to the eye
but allow much to be seen

breaking enigma

she is a clever one
the lock picker
the detective
the inquisitive
the one who finds
the answer in reflections
and the expressions
of the eye

at first light

**if the pen is in my hands
so is the world**

at first light

chapter six: divinity

the working order of
the universe implies
not only intelligence
but intention

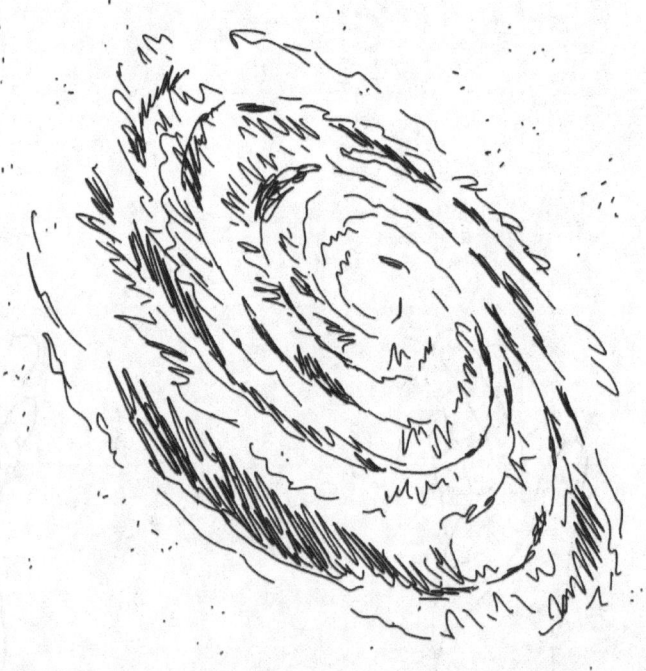

at first light

i can't run back
to where i
came from
because even
walking backwards
on the ground
is moving forward
in time
we are constantly
moving forward
to the future
it's the place we
are destined for
second by second
it is where we are
meant to be

you may be the captain
of your own ship
but even the waves
of the sea move
beyond your control
that is why we must
move with the movements
of life and become
one with them

if the planets can follow
the course of their orbits
and the universe can follow
the course of its expansion
why can't humans follow
the course of their fates

breaking enigma

looking great is a temporary form of affirmation
but a healed heart prevails over any aesthetic
to focus solely on appearance is to reveal
an unusual fixation on the body without
taking into account the balance of the soul

ella zelensky

we stand before
the red sky
and know it
is time
this is the end
this is the
beginning
this is our death
and this is our
awakening
collisions
divisions
and bad decisions
will come back
to haunt us
we will try to run
but our conclusion
has already begun
so we must face
the red sky
and fight not
the urge to cry
because in the end
we will all be
held accountable
in the end
we all die

breaking enigma

it is dark
but you are
near
it hurts
so deeply
but you
are here

some of the things we
desperately want to know
could be the things that
cause us to malfunction

why has humanity given up on the existence of the divine? what is it about divinity that repels people away? humanity has increasingly become afraid of the unknown to such an extent that an accidental beginning of the universe is more palatable than a universe comprised of an intended purpose within its every aspect. perhaps we prefer to think fate is exclusively in our own hands in retaliation to this disturbing unknown. comfort in divine order and its extension to the human race has dwindled as quickly as counter movements for the existence of god have grown. and yet, more than ever, much of humanity has never felt more alone. science has, despite its ground-breaking discoveries, often failed to appease the contemplative soul, of which remains within us all despite our efforts to suppress its persistent curiosity towards a potential divine. any inclination towards such a possibility is considered no less than a threat towards a life of fulfilment and ease – self directed at all costs. but at some point, we yearn for more. our ever-present awe of space and time and the intricate design of universal functionality occupies our minds incessantly, and often obsessively, because we enjoy being in awe. that is, if the awe of it all consists of no ties to a divine explanation. and so we return to our lives, feeding our anxieties with negative hypotheticals and negative decisions to fill precious time, only to skip along paths that meet grim and abrupt ends. convinced prior of the capacity of our human mind to figure out the secret to happiness, we do win some battles alone, whilst other lost battles stand perplexed at our disproven methodology. the personal calculations we made, it seems, did not exactly add up as we had envisioned. and so we return to our contemplation in search of other mysteries to solve in the hopes that we can prove to ourselves that we are the masters of reason, the guardians of truth, the deciders of future. suddenly, and simultaneously, we are also experiencing another wave of spiritual awakening, where people are seeking spirituality. an ever living god, the master of reason, guardian of truth, decider of future fills in the gaps people once feared unresolvable. initiation of prayer soothes the soul as if the person has only just woken up that very day. what they once repelled, they now surrender to, and happily. what was once rejected as an offense to agency is now accepted as a gift to experience. the world follows many religions of all different beliefs and practices, but away from the conflict endures a shared practice to worship what is beyond us, what is out of our control, and is instead within the power of someone or something else. different methods from communities and cultures around the world have often and inevitably still re-aligned with the goal of others to attain a good life, whether now, beyond, or both. intelligence is easy to identify in the universal order, but intent challenges control, and many dream of being in complete control of their life. wherever we are right now in life, and whether we believe in god or not, it remains the conscious and subconscious quest of us all to discover the path towards a good life. and we, as humanity, are not as far away from such a reality as we would first anticipate. this awe – this journey to happiness and contentment – is one we all share.

at first light

breaking enigma

at first light

chapter seven: chemistry

breaking enigma

you need to love to learn
before you learn to love

at first light

**i cannot love someone
who cannot either**

breaking enigma

growth scares you
because deep down
you are dying
to be loved

at first light

i thought you were
pulling my
heart strings
until you unravelled
the rest of me

if what's considered
beautiful
is always changing
then constant must be
the beauty of aging

at first light

every second
is one more
memory

my fingers flit
like a flower
in slow bloom
frame by frame
ticking
i observe the
sunlight
let it highlight
my hand
as i twirl it
around
and i wonder
where you are

ella zelensky

tell me by telling me
not by telling me
without telling me

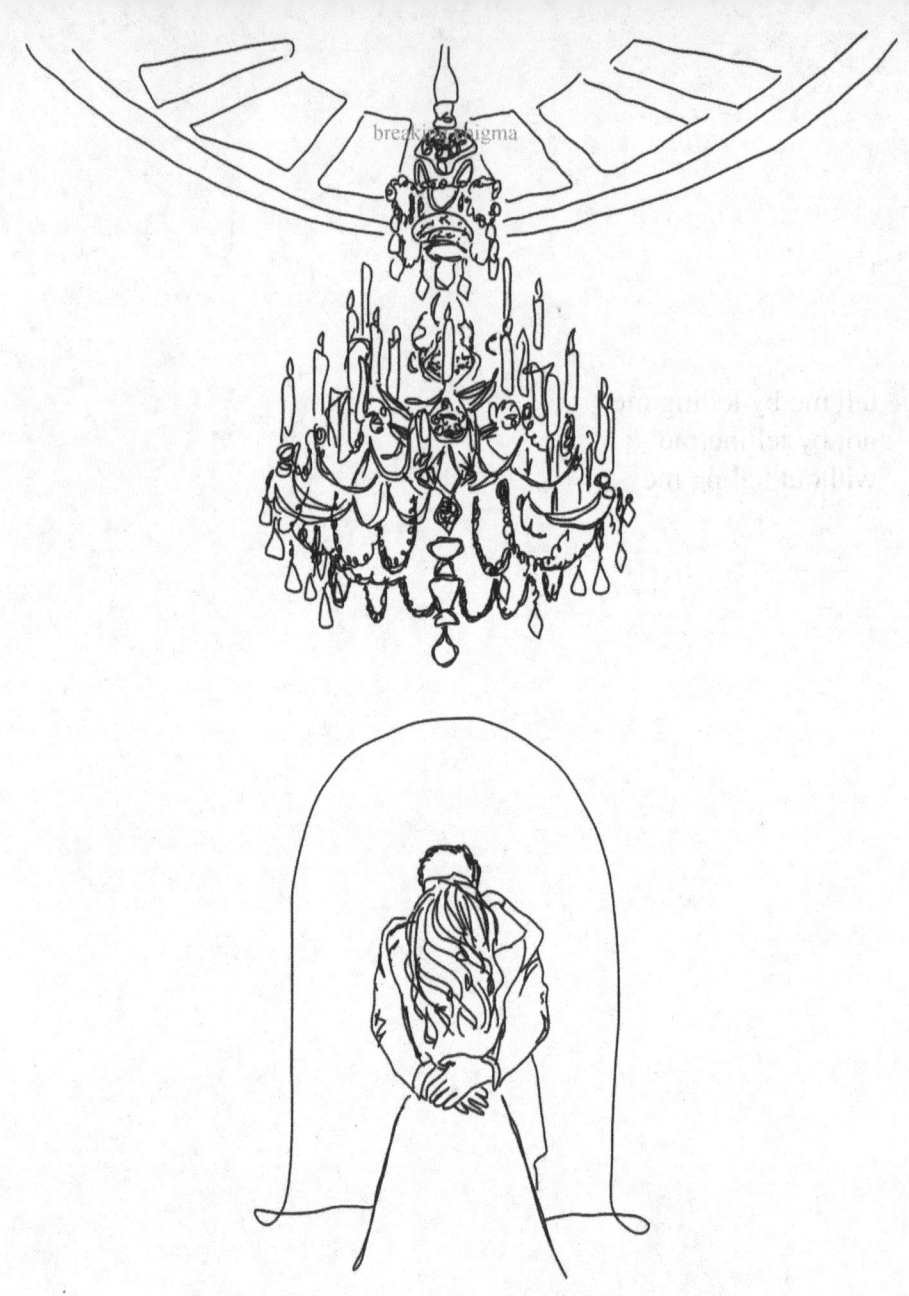

i met you under a chandelier
that cast dreams all around us

ella zelensky

you make me think
i'm dreaming

**you see people differently
when it's raining**

i'm either
wide awake
or fast asleep
in your arms

even the clock is waiting
for us to do something
about this love

ella zelensky

i want you to stay
because you make my day

how can you say
it's beyond us
when it has always
been between us

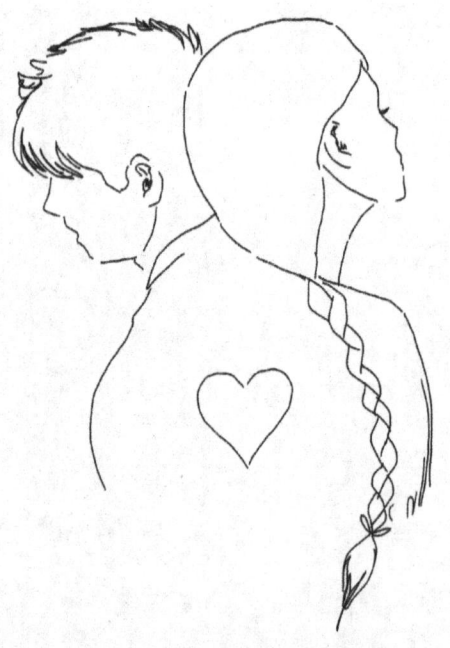

ella zelensky

i was afraid of falling
but not in love with you

the trees canopy
over us
keeping our love
secret to the
outside world

his heart called her name
every day after that day

ella zelensky

when i met you
i knew
the wait was over

a thousand paper butterflies
fell from the sky into my arms
and i knew it was you

ella zelensky

**i didn't know wisdom
could be a person**

breaking enigma

if you can keep up
with my mind
then you have won
my heart

ella zelensky

the eclipse is the
rare kiss
of two lovers
amidst an
audience of stars
savouring
a moment
just a moment
of alignment
before parting
ways again

you were bound
for the wind
and i the ocean
our worlds weren't
meant for each other
how could i breathe
in air and you
in water
how could we survive
in one another's worlds
how could we be
together unless at the
border between us
where i could linger just
under the waves and
you just above them
hands reaching
but never passing
their thresholds
maybe our love is
meant to be at a distance
maybe that's what
love is sometimes
but it doesn't
mean i will ever stop
loving you
even when the world
comes to an end
i will still love you

i looked for you
inside reflections
because our love
seemed only to
exist in different
dimensions

this time
we didn't pass
each other
unconsciously at
the intersection

i await the day
where the question
will you changes
to the answer you will

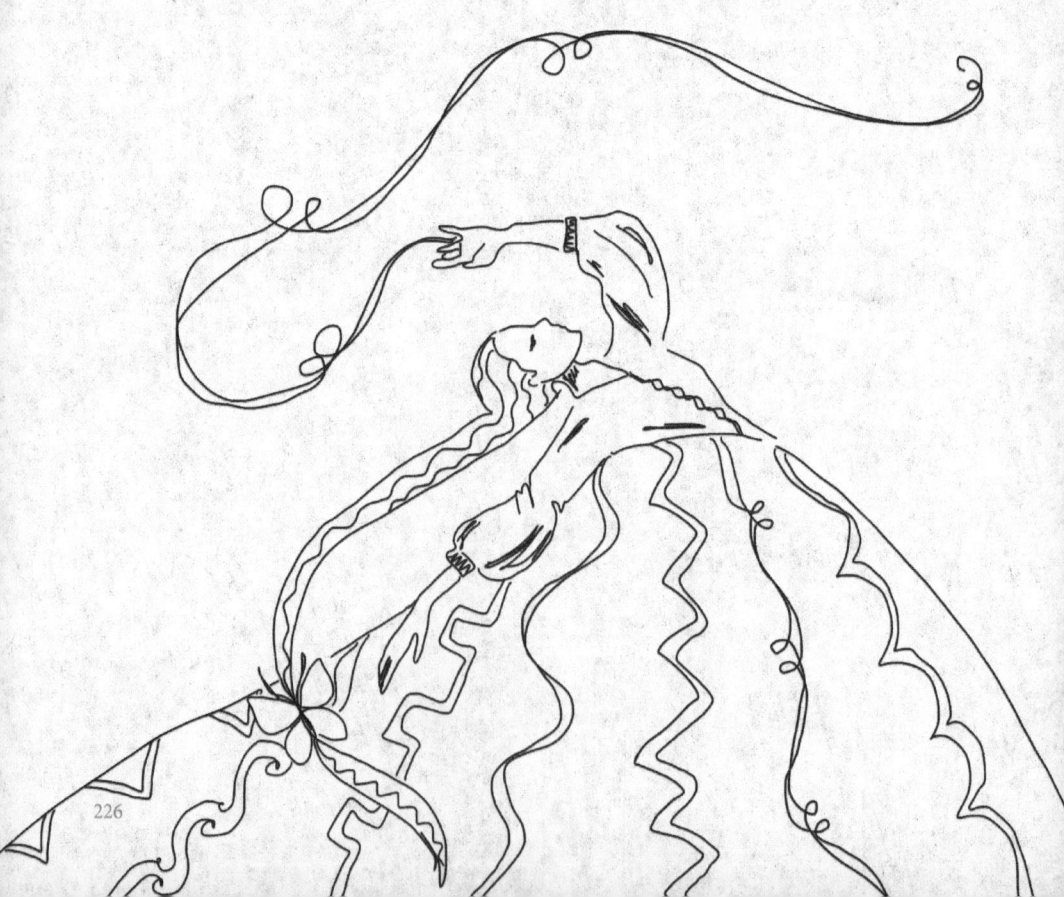

ella zelensky

**come to me
reach for me**

synchronicity
is a love
not always
seen with
the eyes
but deeply felt
with the heart

the heart asks
may i come in
holding the curtain
by its edge
the mind lifts
its head and
gently says yes
and so the two
sit together
i do not think you
irrational the mind says
but i do fear when you
give yourself away
so quickly
the heart smiles
knowingly
i do sometimes it says
but sometimes in life
it's only rational
to love
the mind turns to
the heart faster than
it ever has before
and stares at their hand
until it holds it
and the two become
the best of friends again
in a single moment

we guard our
feelings of love
until the moment
of truth permits
its flow

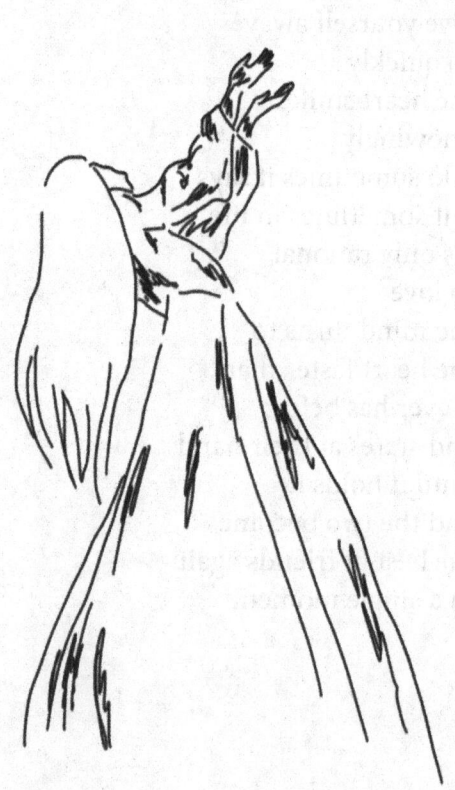

you were halfway
down the stairs
and all i wanted
was to climb the rest
to you
to meet you halfway
as those in love
should

if this is love
isn't it time
as well
if you truly
love me
why wait

ella zelensky

you were elegant
without extravagance
confident without ego
an example for others
without assuming the
podium

the way you
explain life
enchants me

ella zelensky

you only had
to pick me up
for me to
touch the stars

continents away
in the middle
of a meadow
a girl raised her
head to the sky
and prayed for
her love to
show up at
her door

you chased me
with suitcases
in hand
ready to go
on one of
the biggest
adventures of
your life

i fell into madness
as i fell into you

-in sickness and in health

ella zelensky

when i assume
the snow to be
my lifelong habitat
you walk into
my garden
and make petals
fall before my eyes

you still my waters
when they are
writhing with pain
you turn my
storms into gently
falling rain

i think i've loved you
for longer than i've
known you

the game of riddles
between two is fun
but sometimes one just
wants the other to give
an honest answer

ella zelensky

you are not destined to live alone
you are simply afraid that the
right company will change your
entire philosophy on life

when we met our souls reached out with strings
and when we parted we were pulled back
by the knot they made
this love
this connection
was never meant to end

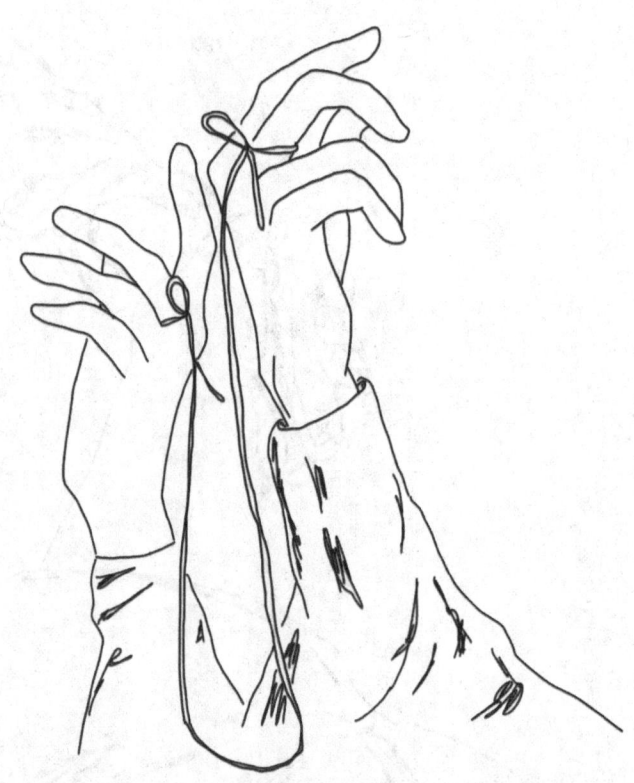

ella zelensky

the concluding word

breaking enigma

Why "breaking enigma"? To be honest, for a moment I wasn't sure why either. It merely appeared in my mind as a spontaneous concept, which slowly began to seem a potentially fitting title for the book. An enigma is a thing we cannot break, decode or unlock. It denotes an impossibility, but it only remains definitional when we observe it within the scope of the dictionary world. In truth, people have been breaking enigmas for thousands of years. In fields of science, technology, mathematics, philosophy, linguistics, communication and many others I can't imagine I'd be able to list completely, we have been stumped by barriers we eventually found a way over. We defied what was once considered impossible and challenged the enigma.

Of course, there are realities out there of certain natures that will likely remain enigmatic. This book is here to assure the audience that that is okay. Not everything is meant to be known. But of the things we are afraid we will never understand or move past in life and suddenly do, time and time again they are a testament to how definitions are constantly being confronted by surprising breakthroughs.

In this way, the book title made the final cut. The title was probably the most casually chosen of the current four books despite its boldly worded allure, since I trusted the quick judgement of my subconscious for it to mean something greater than I could realise in the moment. Spontaneity is among the most powerful of honesties.

So walk into the world and do not be afraid of the unknowns you encounter. You will surely run into some that cause you confusion, anger, pain, disappointment, fear. These unknowns will feel like enigmas that are antagonising or inhibiting you. Not all things in life can be explained concisely enough in a way that is soothing or all-knowing. We will never truly have a complete hold over our lives. But of the things we do find some sort of answer for, these extents can truly be enough if we embrace them. Just as we can see the cup half full, we can recognise glimmers of an answer to still serve as a light in the dark.

You have no idea how many enigmas you have broken in life – in other words, you have proved many assumed impossibilities in this world to be possibilities.

ella zelensky

About the Author

A 2023 graduate from the University of Queensland with a Bachelor of Arts majoring in Anthropology, Ella's studies also included religion, languages, intercultural communication, sociology and film and television. Since she was young, culture, religion, language learning, cinematography and activism have played a major role in her creative work and academic studies. In 2024, Ella starts a new journey commencing in a Postgraduate Bachelor of Law at the Queensland University of Technology.

After struggling with fitting in during her early high school years, writing poetry helped her cope and rise above. Writing eventually became serious to her and she began sharing her work on her social media platform.

Ella published her first poetry book, Little Dreamer in March of 2021, her second book Divine Decree in January 2022 and her third book, At First Light in January 2023.

Her dream to be a humanitarian worker, as well as interests in education, mental health and equality inspire many of her poems and quotes. Through Ella's passion for people, reform, and harmony, she wishes to help others own their identity, take a stand, forgive, unite, and ultimately heal.

In 2018 Ella launched The Leadlight Project, as a creative hub for teens struggling with social isolation and loneliness. The Projects aim, to gather identified teens to develop and create artwork, poetry, short films, and photography to be showcased and celebrated at a collaborative exhibition, scheduled for the 12th of October 2019, in conjunction with QLD Mental Health. Unfortunately, due to ongoing illness, Ella had to place the Project's collaborative Exhibitions on hold. In 2021, the re-formatted project relaunched via a new Shopfront whereby a percentage of sales will be donated to children's charities dear to Ella's heart, including Unicef's Yemen Crisis.

www.ellazelensky.com

breaking enigma ISBN: 978-0-6450978-8-7
breaking enigma e-book ISBN: 978-0-6450978-9-4

© Ella Zelensky, 2024. All rights reserved

www.ingramcontent.com/pod-product-compliance
Lightning Source LLC
Chambersburg PA
CBHW012335300426
44109CB00047B/2549